GOTTHARD DE BEAUCLAIR

Art and literature through typography and design
by Jerry Kelly
with an introduction by Hermann Zapf

THE GROLIER CLUB

15 November 2006 – 12 January 2007
New York

ISBN 0-910672-68-7

GOTTHARD DE BEAUCLAIR was born in Ascona, Switzerland, on 24 July 1907. In Switzerland he was taught in Italian at school until the age of thirteen. He finished his school years in Darmstadt, Germany, where his uncle, the type designer Friedrich Wilhelm Kleukens (who also ran a private press for the Duke Ernst Ludwig of Darmstadt), suggested that he study with Rudolf Koch at the Offenbach Werkstatt. During this training period he studied calligraphy with Koch, printing with the great (but unsung) typographer Prof. Ernst Engel, and composition at the Klingspor typefoundry, where he completed an apprenticeship. De Beauclair's classmates at the Werkstatt included Fritz Kredel, the famous woodcut artist, Herbert Post, designer of several types bearing his name, and Berthold Wolpe, designer of the Albertus and Pegasus types. There he also met the well-known bookbinder, Ignatz Wiemeler, and Ernst Kellner, who later became director of the Offizin Haag-Drugulin in Leipzig. Kellner persuaded de Beauclair to move to Leipzig and work in his printing shop. In Leipzig, de Beauclair again made significant acquaintances, most importantly with Anton Kippenberg who founded Insel Verlag. In 1928 Kippenberg invited de Beauclair to work for him as a book designer. Through this appointment de Beauclair came to know Carl Ernst Poeschel, head of the printing house of Poeschel & Trepte, and Walter Tiemann, noted calligrapher and type designer. It is obvious that exposure to the great printers, calligraphers, and typographers of pre-war Germany provided fertile ground for the growth of de Beauclair's talents.

There is a remarkable duality in de Beauclair's work. Using the most precious materials and the finest craft techniques, he produced limited edition books that rival the finest exemplars of the art of bookmaking, yet he did not shun the production of large commercial editions. Indeed, through his work for Insel, Propyläen, and other commercial publishers, de Beauclair shows that with care an ordinary edition can still be finely produced. Being truly a lover of beautiful books and not merely a devotee of fine materials, he aims to create an exceptional book within the limitations presented to him. His work shows that the most important factor in book manufacture is the intelligent and tasteful handling of typography, materials, and processes. Even though inexpensive, the Insel volumes show care in the minutest details: the typography is readable, elegant, and fresh; the presswork delicate and even; and the board bindings are sometimes elegantly stamped with calligraphic designs, or often have pasted labels on front and spine. Admittedly, few readers appreciate the intricacies of bookmaking, as de Beauclair was well aware, when he wrote:

> As music needs the well trained listener, typography assumes a corresponding ability of the reader to view books in such a way that the shape of the letter and the page, and the general design of the volume, appear not as something incidental and interchangeable but as an optical realization of the words.

The work of de Beauclair stands as a model of fine bookmaking over a broad range of budgets and manufacturing techniques. Of course, credit must be given to the publishers who encouraged his work and were willing to spend slightly more to allow this to be accomplished. There was a time when trade publishers in Germany, such as Insel, Suhrkamp, and Propyläen, would occasionally go to the extra expense of special features such as mould-made paper, a second color on the title page, and fine binding (all of which are incorporated in the sumptuous edition of *Hansen-Bahia* designed by de Beauclair for Hans Christians Verlag and the *Hitda-Codex* for Propyläen). More recently trade book manufacture has sadly declined – even in Germany, where tasteful design and exceptional production quality were the rule rather than the exception well into the late 1960s.

The fine printing being done by private presses today in small pockets on both sides of the Atlantic is often pretentious and almost always prohibitively expensive. However, while we can rejoice in the work of many great book artists currently active in producing both trade and fine publications, it seems the possibilities for working simultaneously on the production of beautiful books in both large commercial runs and fine limited editions have become quite slim. I fear that de Beauclair may have been correct in writing as early as 1966: "An earlier generation of publishers who with shrewd perception worked in close collaboration with an active group of designers has ceased to exist." When he died on 31 March 1992 the situation had not gotten any better; but fortunately de Beauclair and others of his ilk left a body of work in the field of book design that can be appreciated as the pinnacle of an important area of human endeavor.

My thanks for Eric Holzenberg, George Ong, and Hermann Zapf for their valuable suggestions to the text of this publication; and to my wife, Nancy Leo-Kelly, and Hermann Zapf for loaning duplicate copies of several books to the exhibition, thereby enabling the display of additional pages and bindings.

Jerry Kelly

INTRODUCTION

The twentieth century was an era of great letterpress printing and fine edition books. In a few years we will take a much more appreciative look at the well produced books of that time, printed by letterpress. It was also the time of beautiful book designs, with names like Bruce Rogers and William Dwiggins forever connected with examples of careful typography.

In Germany the leading book designer of that time was Gotthard de Beauclair. Unfortunately he is not so well known in America, but perhaps this exhibition of his typographic work might gain more attention for his outstanding publications. The situation in Germany today: very few private presses in Germany are keeping up the tradition of printing from metal type by letterpress. The heritage of the Ernst Ludwig Presse, the Bremer Presse, Walter Tiemann, and Gotthard de Beauclair is in the past. In publishing there is no longer an Anton Kippenberg, an Albert Langen-Müller or a Carl Hanser. The merging of many publishers into big publishing houses has reduced the individuality of the firms; no longer are they guided by personalities who took the risk to discover new talent, or invest in luxurious editions, as in the past. Publishing houses are now managed like any industrial company. Over the last ten years we have seen more and more mass production, with books today being produced as cheaply as possible everywhere, dictated by profit and production costs. The present situation is not the climate for exclusive fine editions done with care in every detail. But today we should still keep up the quality of composition by exploiting the new technology, for now with digital type we are able to get hanging punctuation even in small type sizes and perfectly kerned letters, greater choice of typefaces, and corrections can be made much more easily than before.

Gotthard de Beauclair was trained in the house printing office at the Klingspor foundry in Offenbach. Later he went to Leipzig, to the famous Insel publishing house of Anton Kippenberg. In 1951 he (together with Georg Kurt Schauer) joined the art department of the Stempel typefoundry. I had been there since 1948. The three of us stuck together, for often we had opinions which differed from the management of the firm. Together we fought their mercantile ideas for the press room, getting away from printing just simple advertising and sales material. It was an ideal collaboration, and with de Beauclair, who was a noted poet, the printing soon became much more oriented towards literature.

Gotthard de Beauclair's role at Stempel was mainly to present new typefaces in bookwork, and his critical eye was often the final word regarding many typographic issues.

In all the years we worked together de Beauclair and I never had any disagreements, for he was a true professional. I enjoyed working with him at the Stempel foundry very much, and also at the Insel Verlag, for which he was production manager. Insel was originally located in Leipzig, but after the War they moved to Wiesbaden in the West. De Beauclair moved to the West in 1946, for he could not live under the Communist regime in East-Germany.

At Insel he was responsible for the "Insel-Bücherei" (Insel Editions), small books only 12 x 18 cm (4¾ x 7 inches) in size. But each volume was produced with exceptional care in order to achieve the highest quality in illustration and text composition. Today the little books of the classic "Insel-Bücherei" are collectors items. Gotthard de Beauclair received a gold medal at the World's Fair in Paris 1937 for his designs for the "Insel-Bücherei."

He discovered then-unknown book illustrators such as Fritz Kredel and others, giving them the opportunity to illustrate entire books in their preferred techniques, such as woodcuts, lithography, or etching. He was very helpful to Kredel particularly after he emigrated to New York (it was really not easy during the National-Socialist era in Germany to transfer money from Germany to the USA). Even during the very hard times after the War de Beauclair continued to commission illustrations from living artists. At that time many other publishers copied nineteenth century wood engravings, etc., as cheap sources so that they would not have to pay for contemporary work.

Within the Stempel foundry in Frankfurt Gotthard de Beauclair established the Trajanus Presse to print special fine editions, mostly illustrated. The editions were produced under the generous conditions of the typefoundry. He was known to be very careful in every detail of hand composition, and also in preparing trial pages to achieve the best arrangement for a job. Most often he designed books without any time limits, for he never liked to work under a deadline for these books. A few famous titles issued by the Trajanus Presse are Gertrud von le Fort's *Plus Ultra*, printed in Diotima and bound by Gudrun von Hesse (1953); Werner Bergengruen's *Die drei Falken*, set in Palatino roman with color woodcuts by Felix Hoffmann (1956); Hugo von Hofmannsthal *Lucidor*, set in original Janson roman, and also with woodcuts by Felix Hoffmann (1959); *Das Evangelium des Johannes* in Greek and German, set in Aldus roman and Heraklit Greek (1960); and Aristophanes' *Die Frösche* with wood engravings by Imre Reiner (1961). After 1962 he founded a new enterprise: "Ars librorum." The idea was to print exclusive publications, but now independent from the D. Stempel AG typefoundry. There he produced expensive books to the highest standards, without any commercial restrictions. He chose the best papers for his editions, as well as the best binders, like Willy Pingel in Heidelberg and Hellmuth Halbach in Königstein, and the finest printers in Germany, such as Ludwig Oehms in Frankfurt or the Eggebrecht Press in Mainz. The Ars Librorum editions books were highlights of German book production after the War. A few titles are: Sophocles' *Antigone,* with ten etchings by Eduard Bargheer, composed in Bell Roman (1967) *Amor und Psyche* with etchings by Felix Hoffmann, set in Palatino (1963); Plato's *Das Gastmal oder Über die Liebe,* printed from Bembo type with etchings by Heinz Battke (1965).

A complete collection of all books designed by Gotthard de Beauclair is in the "Ars Librorum Collection" of the Herzog August Bibliothek in Wolfenbüttel, Germany. A publication about his life and work, *Gotthard de Beauclair. Buchgestalter, Lyriker, Verleger 1907–1992,* was published in 1996 by Gert Fischer and Heinz Richter (Rheinlandia: Klaus Walterscheid in Siegburg, Germany). This book shows many beautiful illustrations of de Beauclair's work in actual size.

Aside from his many book designs Gotthard de Beauclair is well known for his poetry. He represented the very rare combination of an outstanding book designer and a poet who knows the importance of words – their color, and the expressive power behind them, as articulated in poetry. Lucky are those books collectors who have in their collections editions designed by Gotthard de Beauclair – they are treasures of the best produced editions of the last century.

Hermann Zapf *August 2006*

I BEGINNINGS

De Beauclair was a student of Rudolf Koch at the Offenbach Werkstatt. During this training period he studied calligraphy with Koch, printing with Ernst Engel, and composition at the Klingspor typefoundry, where he completed an apprenticeship. In 1928 Anton Kippenberg, head of the Insel Verlag in Leipzig, invited de Beauclair to work for him as a book designer. Through this appointment de Beauclair came to know key suppliers to Insel: Carl Ernst Poeschel, head of the printing house of Poeschel & Trepte, and Walter Tiemann, noted calligrapher, book designer and type designer. Leipzig, the pre-war center of the German book trade, was destroyed during World War II. The German publishing industry emerged from the war in a state of chaos. De Beauclair managed to escape with a single suitcase into the British zone, but he was ill and starving. His first communication from the outside world was a food parcel from his former Werkstatt classmate and fellow typographer, Henri Friedlaender, who had suffered through the painful years of the German occupation in Holland before establishing himself as a fine printer in Israel.

1 . Gotthard de Beauclair, DIE ALTSCHRIFT
   VON HERBERT POST
   in *Rudolf Koch und sein Kreis*
   Leipzig, Archiv für Buchgewerbe und Gebrauchsgraphik. 1933
   Specimen setting designed by de Beauclair in Post Titling.

2 . Gotthard de Beauclair, IN MEMORIAM
   Dessau, Karl Rauch Verlag. 1942

3 . Gotthard de Beauclair, DAS VERBORGENE HEIL
   Gedichte 1942 bis 1946
   Krefeld, Scherpe Verlag. 1946

II INSEL VERLAG

After the war, de Beauclair's typographic career slowly resumed its true course. In 1952 he became the head of book design at the newly formed West German branch of Insel Verlag, in Wiesbaden, later in Frankfurt. Interestingly, de Beauclair was offered a key editorial position at Insel, but turned it down in favor of the design leadership. Many know and admire the beautiful yet inexpensive Insel publications (including the well-known Insel-Bücherei series), but few are aware that de Beauclair designed most of these volumes throughout the 1950s and '60s. The head of the publishing house, Anton Kippenberg, did not wish for the designer's name to appear in his publications, hence the anonymity. Also anonymous were many calligraphic stamping designs for the covers by Hermann Zapf – commissioned by de Beauclair – which grace many an Insel volume.

4. Rainer Maria Rilke, BRIEFE ÜBER CÉZANNE
   Wiesbaden, Insel Verlag (Insel Bücherei). 1952

5. DIE GESCHICHTE VON AUCASSIN UND NICOLETTE.
   Woodcuts by Fritz Kredel, hand colored.
   Leipzig, Insel Verlag. 1955

6. Rainer Maria Rilke, SÄMLICHE WERKE (6 volumes)
   Wiesbaden, Insel Verlag 1955

7. HAIKU: JAPANISCHE DREIZEILER
   Frankfurt, Insel Verlag. 1960

8. DEUTSCHE GEDICHTE
   Selected by Katharina Kippenberg (the wife of the publisher).
   Frankfurt, Insel Verlag. 1963

INSEL BÜCHEREI (items 9–17)

9. Fritz Kredel, DAS KLEINE BUCH DER VÖGEL UND
   NESTER
   Leipzig, Insel Verlag. [1935]

10. DEUTSCHE HOLZSCHNITTE
    DES XX. JAHRHUNDERTS
    Wiesbaden, Insel Verlag. 1955

11. Hugo von Hofmannstahl, GEDICHTE
    Wiesbaden, Insel Verlag. 1955

12. Walther von der Vogelweide, GEDICHTE
    Wiesbaden, Insel Verlag. 1955

13. DER ACKERMANN UND DER TOD
    Frankfurt, Insel Verlag. 1957

14. GOETHES SCHÖNSTE BRIEFE
    Wiesbaden, Insel Verlag. 1957

15. Scholem-Alejchem, EINE HOCHZEIT OHNE
    MUSIKANTEN
    Frankfurt, Insel Verlag. 1961
    Illustrations by Ben Shahn

16. Christians von Hofmannswaldau, HELDEN-BRIEFE
    Frankfurt, Insel Verlag. 1962

17. Heinrich Böll, IM TAL DER DONNERNDEN HUFE
    Frankfurt, Insel Verlag. 1962

DUST JACKETS FOR INSEL (items 18–22)

18. Rainer Maria Rilke, DUINESER ELEGIEN
    Wiesbaden, Insel Verlag. 1955

19. LOB DES ALTERS
    Wiesbaden, Insel Verlag. 1957

20. DEUTSCHE ERZÄHLER
    Wiesbaden, Insel Verlag. 1958

21. Adalbert Stifter, LEBEN UND WERK
    Frankfurt, Insel Verlag. 1962

22. DEUTSCHE GEDICHTE
    Frankfurt, Insel Verlag. 1963

III OTHER PUBLISHERS

In addition to his work for Insel, de Beauclair was commissioned to design volumes published by many other prominent German publishers, including Propyläen, Scherpe, Büchergilde Gutenberg, and other commercial firms. In his work for these trade publishers de Beauclair shows that with care an ordinary edition can be finely done. Desirous of producing beautiful books in all forms, not only fine editions, he created exceptional books within the limitations presented to him. His work shows that the most important factor in book manufacture is not budget, but the intelligent and tasteful handling of typography, materials, and processes.

23. Gotthard de Beauclair, BLÜHENDES MOOS
    With initials by Johann Zainer re-cut in wood by Josef Weisz.
    Privately printed, 1953

24. Friedrich Rückert, GEDÄCHTNIS UND VERMÄCHTNIS
    Frankfurt, Fränkische Bibliophilen-Gesellschaft. 1955
    1000 copies

25. KOSTBARKEITEN, Aus Chemie und Technik vergangener Jahrhunderte
    Wiesbaden-Biebrich, Chemische Werke Albert. 1958

26. Hermann Schnitzler, RHEINISCHE SCHATZKAMMER
    Düsseldorf, L. Schwann. 1959

27. Boccaccio, DIE GEDICHTE VON FRIEDRICH DEGLI ALBERIGHI UND SEINEM FALKEN
    Büttenfabrik Hahnemühle. 1959

28. DIE HEILIGE SCHRIFT
Württembergische Bibelanstalt. [N.D.]

29. HANSEN-BAHIA, Stationen und Wegmarken eines Holzschneiders
Hamburg, Hans Christians Verlag. 1960
900 copies

30. Xenophon, DIE WAFFEN DES EROS
With thirteen illustrations by Giacomo Manzù.
Berlin & Frankfurt, Propyläen Verlag. 1968

31. Arthur Schnitzler, FRÜHE GEDICHTE
Berlin, Propyläen Verlag. 1969

32. PROPYLÄEN KUNSTGESCHCHTE
Berlin, Propyläen Verlag. 1974
One volume of an extensive, multi-volume history of world art.

33. DER DARMSTÄDTER HITDA-CODEX
Berlin, Propyläen Verlag. 1968
450 copies.

IV THE STEMPEL TYPEFOUNDRY

In 1951 de Beauclair became a typographer and design consultant to the Stempel typefoundry in Frankfurt. During his years at Stempel, de Beauclair developed an important working relationship with Hermann Zapf and Georg Kurt Schauer, who were also employed by the foundry. Stempel had an exceptional commitment to technical and artistic excellence; as a result, the type designs, specimens, and fine books that Stempel issued through the efforts of these men dramatically influenced the course of modern typography. The Palatino, Diotima, and Optima types, to name just a few, were extraordinary, being calligraphically based faces which were serviceable, not as idiosyncratic (and thereby restricted in usefulness) as previous German typefaces with calligraphic origins. At Stempel de Beauclair was advisor to several type design projects. He suggested that Hermann Zapf design a type in the same family as Palatino but more suited to book work; the result was the Aldus font. He invited Jan Tschichold to develop a type based on Garamond and suitable for photocomposition, Linotype, Monotype, or for hand setting; this became the popular Sabon font. De Beauclair was also instrumental in the Balzac font, a brush script type designed by Johannes Boehland.

34. GARAMOND, Die zeitlos schöne Schrift
    Frankfurt, D. Stempel AG [n.d.]

35. ALDUS & PALATINO, Die Schrift im Buch
    Frankfurt, D. Stempel AG [n.d.]

36. Gotthard de Beauclair, SUITE FÜR EURALDA
    Frankfurt, D. Stempel AG. 1953

37. Ada Battke, PALOMAR
    Frankfurt, D. Stempel AG. 1958
    250 copies

38. Gertrud von le Fort, PLUS ULTRA
    Frankfurt, Trajanus Presse. 1953
    500 copies
    The first book printed in Diotima Roman, designed by
    Gudrun Zapf von Hesse

39. R. M. Rilke, VOM ALLEINSEIN
    Frankfurt, Trajanus Presse. 1951
    500 copies
    The first book printed in Palatino italic, designed by
    Hermann Zapf.

40. DER ROMAN VON TRISTAN UND ISOLDE
    Frankfurt, Trajanus Presse. 1966
    300 copies
    With hand-colored woodcuts by Fritz Kredel. The first book
    printed in Sabon roman, designed by Jan Tschichold.

V TRAJANUS PRESSE

The most important book works resulting from de Beauclair's association with Stempel are the sixteen books published under the imprint of the Trajanus Presse. The Presse was the property of Stempel with de Beauclair acting as editor, publisher, and designer (with one exception: Hermann Zapf's *Feder und Stichel*). Although he left his position at Stempel in 1959 to devote more time to Insel and other work, de Beauclair continued to work on the Trajanus Presse books until 1968. Several of these books featured the first use of a new typeface manufactured by Stempel, and therefore are listed elsewhere in this catalogue (Palatino italic: Rilke, *Vom Alleinsein* – no. 39; Diotima: von le Fort, *Plus Ultra* – no. 38; and Sabon: *Der Roman von Tristan und Isolde* – no. 40).

41. Johann Peter Hebel, SELTSAMER SPAZIERRITT
    Frankfurt, Trajanus Presse. 1951
    The first Trajanus Presse book, set in original Janson italic.

42. Giovanni di Boccaccio, DIE NYMPHE VON FIESOLE
    Frankfurt, Trajanus Presse. 1953
    38 woodcuts by Felix Hoffmann. Set in Janson types.
    300 copies

43. DAS EVANGELIUM JOHANNES
    Frankfurt, Trajanus Presse. 1960
    150 copies
    Set in Aldus, Heraklit, Palatino, and Michelangelo (all Stempel types designed by Hermann Zapf).

44. Werner Bergengruen, DIE DREI FALKEN

With color woodcuts by Felix Hoffmann.
Frankfurt, Trajanus Presse. 1956
350 copies

45. MOZARTS BRIEFE AUS PARIS

Frankfurt, Trajanus Presse. 1963
875 copies

46. Jean Moréas, AUSGEWÄHLTE GEDICHTE

Etchings by Willy Meter-Osberg.
Frankfurt, Trajanus Presse. 1972
85 copies
The last Trajanus Presse book, set in Caslon (Stempel was a distrib-
utor of the Caslon types, which were cast by the Haas Typefoundry
in Switzerland from electrotypes of the original matrices).

VI ARS LIBRORUM

In addition to the Trajanus Presse books, de Beauclair produced fine editions under two other imprints: Ars Librorum and Edition de Beauclair. The Ars Librorum books are illustrated in the tradition of the French livres d'artiste, but without the overemphasis on the pictures to the detriment of the text evident in many of the French publications. Here, text and illustration are each beautiful in their own right, and both work together harmoniously. The craftsmanship, materials, and even the general overall aesthetic of these editions are not dissimilar to those of the Trajanus Presse, but Verlag Ars Librorum was de Beauclair's own independent imprint. Therefore, he could have the freedom to use a wider range of typefaces and content than at the Trajanus Presse, which was part of the Stempel typefoundry.

47. DAS UNSCHÄTZBARE SCHLOSS IN DER AFRIKANISCHEN HÖHLE XA XA

Illustrations by Wilfried Blecher.
Frankfurt, Ars Librorum. 1962
900 copies

48. LAUDATE DOMINUM

Frankfurt, Ars Librorum. 1963
950 copies

49. Apulejus, AMOR UND PSYCHE

Etchings by Felix Hoffmann.
Frankfurt, Ars Librorum. 1963
175 copies

50. Paul Appel, GARTEN IM HERBST
Lithographs by Imre Reiner.
Frankfurt, Ars Librorum. 1964
165 copies

51. HÖLDERLINS VERSTUMMEN
Frankfurt, Ars Librorum. 1964
300 copies

52. Plato, DAS GASTMAHL
Etchings by Heinz Battke.
Frankfurt, Ars Librorum. 1965
300 copies

In 1966 the first Edition de Beauclair was published. These large-format publications provided a forum for the visual artist; the illustrations are the focus and the text is secondary. The thirteen Edition de Beauclair titles contain lithographs, etchings, or drypoints by such noted artists as Max Pfeiffer Watenphul, Oskar Kokoschka, Giorgio de Chirico, and Jean Moréas.

53. Giuseppe Ungaretti, NOTIZEN DES ALTEN
    Lithographs by Pericle Fazzini.
    Frankfurt, Edition de Beauclair. 1967
    200 copies

54. Baha'u'llah, HIDDEN WORDS FROM THE ARABIC
    Serigraph by Mark Tobey.
    Frankfurt, Edition de Beauclair. 1974
    100 copies

55. Berthold Brecht, LEGENDE VON DER ENTSTEHUNG DES BUCHES TAO TE KING
    Lithographic portrait by Gustav Seitz.
    Frankfurt, Edition de Beauclair. 1967
    235 copies

VIII COLLABORATION WITH ARTISTS

A key aspect of de Beauclair's work was his collaboration with artists, as can be seen from several of the titles published by him, and shown elsewhere in this exhibition. Well-known painters and printmakers such as Imre Reiner and Mark Tobey were personal friends of his. An exhibition at the Klingspor Museum in Offenbach, Germany, in 1982 was devoted entirely to de Beauclair's work with his artist friends (see item 60).

56. Rudolf Borchardt, DAS BUCH JORAM
    Lithographs by Hans Fronius.
    Frankfurt, Trajanus Presse. 1962
    225 copies

57. GENESIS
    Color woodcuts by Felix Hoffmann.
    Frankfurt, Ars Librorum. 1965
    475 copies

58. Sophokles, ANTIGONE
    Etchings by Eduard Bargheer.
    Frankfurt, Ars Librorum. 1967
    200 copies

59. ÄSOPISCHE FABELN
    Linoleum cuts by Imre Reiner.
    Frankfurt, Trajanus Presse. 1968
    350 copies

60. GOTTHARD DE BEAUCLAIR UND SEINE
KÜNSTLERFREUNDE
Offenbach, Klingspor Museum. 1982
Exhibition poster, with an illustration by Mark Tobey.

61. Aristophanes, DIE FRÖSCHE
12 etchings by Oskar Kokoschka.
Frankfurt, Ars Librorum. 1968
190 copies; 25 *hors commerce* lettered A–Z

IX MISCELLANEOUS

62. LIBER LIBRORUM
Stockholm, privately printed. 1955
A collection of specimen Bible pages, designed by various typographers from around the world. De Beauclair contributed four samples to the project.

63. DIE SCHÖNSTEN DEUTSCHE BÜCHER
[various years]
The German equivalent of the "AIGA Fifty Books of the Year." From 1950 through 1975 – a golden age for modern German book design – Gotthard de Beauclair was honored with more selections than any other designer.

64. GOTTHARD DE BEAUCLAIR, MODERN GERMAN BOOK DESIGNER
London, Monotype Corporation. 1962

65. VERLAG ARS LIBRORUM · TRAJANUS-PRESSE
Catalogue of private press publications by de Beauclair
Frankfurt, [N.D.]

66. GOTTHARD DE BEAUCLAIR, LEBEN UND WERK
Siegburg, Rheinlandia Verlag. 1996

ILLUSTRATIONS

HAIKU *Japanische Dreizeiler*

AUSGEWÄHLT UND AUS DEM URTEXT

ÜBERTRAGEN VON JAN ULENBROOK

IM INSEL-VERLAG · MCMLX

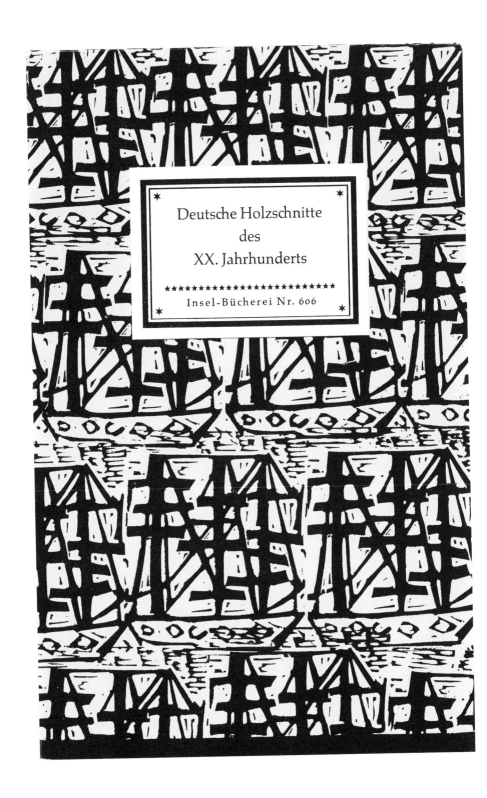

Deutsche Holzschnitte
des
XX. Jahrhunderts

★★★★★★★★★★★★★★★★★★★★★★★★★★

Insel-Bücherei Nr. 606

HERRN CHRISTIANS

VON HOFMANNSWALDAU

SINNREICHE

Helden=Briefe

VERLIEBTER PERSONEN

VON STANDE

IM INSEL-VERLAG

ADALBERT
STIFTERS
LEBEN UND
WERK

IN·BRIEFEN UND
DOKUMENTEN

INSEL

Rainer Maria Rilke

—

Duineser Elegien

IM INSEL-VERLAG

München, am Allerheiligentage 1915

Es ist mir, Herr Jomar Förste, wie ein Vorwurf, zu
sehen, daß Ihr guter Brief, den ich wieder las, das
Datum des 28ten August trägt. Hab ich so lange
nicht geantwortet?
Das ist das einzige Gute dieser ins unverantwort-
lichste Geschehn verpflichteten Wochen, Monate,
daß sie rascher als andere hinzustürzen scheinen, als
wünschten sie selber nichts, wie vorbei zu sein und
fürchteten, man könne sie fragen, wohin sie's treiben.
Wenigstens mir hier entgeht Zeit um Zeit, die Un-
wirklichkeit, die das alles für mich hat, trägt wohl
dazu bei, es dahinzuwirbeln: Denn wo wäre ein
Tag, den man faßte, sich zu eigen machte, im genauen
geistigen Sinne? Es sind nur unfaßliche da.
Das Abseits-Sein, von dem Sie in Ihrem Briefe
erzählen, ist mir, der ich nie eine andere Einrichtung
gekannt habe, nichts Verwunderliches. Wie nun

GARAMOND

Die
zeitlos schöne
Schrift

D. STEMPEL AG
SCHRIFTGIESSEREI
FRANKFURT A. M.

DER DARMSTÄDTER HITDA-CODEX

BILDER UND ZIERSEITEN AUS DER
HANDSCHRIFT 1640 DER HESSISCHEN LANDES-
UND HOCHSCHULBIBLIOTHEK

MIT ERLÄUTERUNGEN VON PETER BLOCH
UND EINEM VORWORT VON
ERICH ZIMMERMANN

BERLIN
PROPYLÄEN VERLAG

FRIEDRICH RÜCKERT

GEDÄCHTNIS UND VERMÄCHTNIS

EINGELEITET

UND HERAUSGEGEBEN

VON

GEORG SCHNEIDER

—

FRÄNKISCHE

BIBLIOPHILEN-GESELLSCHAFT

DIE NYMPHE

VON

FIESOLE

sandt hast. ²⁶Und ich habe ihnen deinen Namen kundgetan und will ihn kundtun, damit die Liebe, mit der du mich liebst, sei in ihnen und ich in ihnen.

18 Da Jesus solches geredet hatte, ging er hinaus mit seinen Jüngern über den Bach Kidron; da war ein Garten, darein ging Jesus und seine Jünger. ²Judas aber, der ihn verriet, wußte den Ort auch, denn Jesus versammelte sich oft daselbst mit seinen Jüngern. ³Da nun Judas zu sich genommen hatte die Schar der Kriegsknechte und die Diener der Hohenpriester und Pharisäer, kommt er dahin mit Fackeln, Lampen und mit Waffen. ⁴Da nun Jesus wußte alles, was ihm begegnen sollte, ging er hinaus und sprach zu ihnen: Wen suchet ihr? ⁵Sie antworteten ihm: Jesus von Nazareth. Er spricht zu ihnen: Ich bin's! Judas aber, der ihn verriet, stand auch bei ihnen. ⁶Als nun Jesus zu ihnen sprach: Ich bin's! wichen sie zurück und fielen zu Boden. ⁷Da fragte er sie abermals: Wen suchet ihr? Sie aber sprachen: Jesus von Nazareth. ⁸Jesus antwortete: Ich habe es euch gesagt, daß ich's bin. Suchet ihr denn mich, so lasset diese gehen! ⁹auf daß das Wort erfüllt würde, welches er gesagt hatte: Ich habe derer keinen verloren, die du mir gegeben hast. ¹⁰Da hatte Simon Petrus ein Schwert und zog es heraus und schlug nach des Hohenpriesters Knecht und hieb ihm sein rechtes Ohr ab. Und der Knecht hieß Malchus. ¹¹Da sprach Jesus zu Petrus: Stecke dein Schwert in die Scheide! Soll ich den Kelch nicht trinken, den mir mein Vater gegeben hat?

¹²Die Schar aber und der Oberhauptmann und die Diener der Juden nahmen Jesus und banden ihn ¹³und führten ihn zuerst zu Hannas; der war der Schwiegervater des Kaiphas, welcher des Jahres Hoherpriester war. ¹⁴Es war aber Kaiphas, der den Juden geraten hatte, es wäre gut, daß EIN Mensch stürbe für das Volk. ¹⁵Simon Petrus aber folgte Jesus nach und ein anderer Jünger. Dieser Jünger war dem Hohenpriester bekannt und ging mit Jesus hinein in des Hohenpriesters Palast. ¹⁶Petrus aber stand draußen vor der Tür. Da ging der andere Jünger, der dem Hohenpriester bekannt war, hinaus und redete mit der Türhüterin und führte Petrus hinein. ¹⁷Da sprach die Magd, die Türhüterin, zu Petrus: Bist du nicht auch einer von den Jüngern dieses Menschen? Er sprach: Ich bin's nicht. ¹⁸Es standen aber die

τοι ἔγνωσαν ὅτι σύ με ἀπέστειλας· καὶ ἐγνώρισα αὐτοῖς τὸ ὄνομά σου καὶ γνωρίσω, ἵνα ἡ ἀγάπη ἣν ἠγάπησάς με ἐν αὐτοῖς ᾖ κἀγὼ ἐν αὐτοῖς.

Ταῦτα εἰπὼν Ἰησοῦς ἐξῆλθεν σὺν τοῖς μαθηταῖς αὐτοῦ πέραν τοῦ χειμάρρου τοῦ Κεδρών, ὅπου ἦν κῆπος, εἰς ὃν εἰσῆλθεν αὐτὸς καὶ οἱ μαθηταὶ αὐτοῦ. ᾔδει δὲ καὶ Ἰούδας ὁ παραδιδοὺς αὐτὸν τὸν τόπον, ὅτι πολλάκις συνήχθη Ἰησοῦς ἐκεῖ μετὰ τῶν μαθητῶν αὐτοῦ. ὁ οὖν Ἰούδας λαβὼν τὴν σπεῖραν καὶ ἐκ τῶν ἀρχιερέων καὶ ἐκ τῶν Φαρισαίων ὑπηρέτας ἔρχεται ἐκεῖ μετὰ φανῶν καὶ λαμπάδων καὶ ὅπλων. Ἰησοῦς οὖν εἰδὼς πάντα τὰ ἐρχόμενα ἐπ᾽ αὐτὸν ἐξῆλθεν καὶ λέγει αὐτοῖς· τίνα ζητεῖτε; ἀπεκρίθησαν αὐτῷ· Ἰησοῦν τὸν Ναζωραῖον. λέγει αὐτοῖς· ἐγώ εἰμι. εἱστήκει δὲ καὶ Ἰούδας ὁ παραδιδοὺς αὐτὸν μετ᾽ αὐτῶν. ὡς οὖν εἶπεν αὐτοῖς· ἐγώ εἰμι, ἀπῆλθαν εἰς τὰ ὀπίσω καὶ ἔπεσαν χαμαί. πάλιν οὖν ἐπηρώτησεν αὐτούς· τίνα ζητεῖτε; οἱ δὲ εἶπαν· Ἰησοῦν τὸν Ναζωραῖον. ἀπεκρίθη Ἰησοῦς· εἶπον ὑμῖν ὅτι ἐγώ εἰμι· εἰ ἐμὲ ζητεῖτε, ἄφετε τούτους ὑπάγειν· ἵνα πληρωθῇ ὁ λόγος ὃν εἶπεν, ὅτι οὓς δέδωκάς μοι, οὐκ ἀπώλεσα ἐξ αὐτῶν οὐδένα. Σίμων οὖν Πέτρος ἔχων μάχαιραν εἵλκυσεν αὐτὴν καὶ ἔπαισεν τοῦ ἀρχιερέως δοῦλον καὶ ἀπέκοψεν αὐτοῦ τὸ ὠτάριον τὸ δεξιόν· ἦν δὲ ὄνομα τῷ δούλῳ Μάλχος. εἶπεν οὖν ὁ Ἰησοῦς τῷ Πέτρῳ· βάλε τὴν μάχαιραν εἰς τὴν θήκην· τὸ ποτήριον ὃ δέδωκέν μοι ὁ πατήρ, οὐ μὴ πίω αὐτό;
Ἡ οὖν σπεῖρα καὶ ὁ χιλίαρχος καὶ οἱ ὑπηρέται τῶν Ἰουδαίων συνέλαβον τὸν Ἰησοῦν καὶ ἔδησαν αὐτὸν καὶ ἤγαγον πρὸς Ἄνναν πρῶτον· ἦν γὰρ πενθερὸς τοῦ Καϊάφα, ὃς ἦν ἀρχιερεὺς τοῦ ἐνιαυτοῦ ἐκείνου· ἦν δὲ Καϊάφας ὁ συμβουλεύσας τοῖς Ἰουδαίοις ὅτι συμφέρει ἕνα ἄνθρωπον ἀποθανεῖν ὑπὲρ τοῦ λαοῦ. Ἠκολούθει δὲ τῷ Ἰησοῦ Σίμων Πέτρος καὶ ἄλλος μαθητής. ὁ δὲ μαθητὴς ἐκεῖνος ἦν γνωστὸς τῷ ἀρχιερεῖ, καὶ συνεισῆλθεν τῷ Ἰησοῦ εἰς τὴν αὐλὴν τοῦ ἀρχιερέως, ὁ δὲ Πέτρος εἱστήκει πρὸς τῇ θύρᾳ ἔξω. ἐξῆλθεν οὖν ὁ μαθητὴς ὁ ἄλλος ὁ γνωστὸς τοῦ ἀρχιερέως καὶ εἶπεν τῇ θυρωρῷ, καὶ εἰσήγαγεν τὸν Πέτρον. λέγει οὖν τῷ Πέτρῳ ἡ παιδίσκη ἡ θυρωρός· μὴ καὶ σὺ ἐκ τῶν μαθητῶν εἶ τοῦ ἀνθρώπου τούτου;

PSALM 112 *Lobsingt, ihr Diener des Herrn, / lobsinget dem Namen des Herrn! / Der Name des Herrn sei gepriesen / jetzt und in Ewigkeit. / Vom Aufgang der Sonne bis an den Niedergang: / der Name des Herrn sei gepriesen! / Erhaben ist der Herr über all die Völker, / erhaben seine Herrlichkeit über die Himmel.*
Wer ist wie der Herr, unser Gott, der thront in der Höhe, / der niederschaut auf Himmel und Erde? / Den Geringen hebt er empor aus dem Staub, / aus der Verachtung erhebt er den Armen. / Er verleiht ihm Sitz bei den Fürsten, / bei den Edelsten seines Volkes. / Die kinderlos war, läßt er wohnen im Hause / als Mutter, froh ihrer Kinder.

PSALM 113 *Als Israel zog aus Ägypten, / Jakobs Stamm aus dem fremden Volk: / zum Heiligtum ward Juda dem Herrn, / zu seinem Reiche ward Israel.*
Das Meer sah es und floh, / der Jordan wandte rückwärts den Lauf. / Die Berge hüpften den Widdern gleich, / wie junge Lämmer die Hügel.
Was ist dir, Meer, daß du fliehst? / Jordan, was wendest du rückwärts den Lauf? / Ihr Berge, was hüpfet ihr gleich den Widdern, / wie junge Lämmer ihr Hügel?
Erde, erbebe vor dem Anblick des Herrn, / vor Jakobs Gott, vor seinem heiligen Antlitz! / Der den Felsen gewandelt zum Weiher, / zur strömenden Quelle den Stein.
Nicht uns, o Herr, nicht uns, / Ehre verleih deinem Namen, / um deiner Gnade willen und deiner Treue. / Warum sollen sagen die Heiden: / Wo ist nun ihr Gott?
Unser Gott ist im Himmel; / alles, was er wollte, er hat es vollbracht. / Ihre Götzen aber sind Silber und Gold, / gebildet von

Laudate pueri Dominum laudate nomen Domini. Sit nomen Domini benedictum; ex hoc nunc et usque in saeculum. A solis ortu usque ad occasum; laudabile nomen Domini. Excelsus super omnes gentes Dominus; et super caelos gloria eius. Quis sicut Dominus Deus noster qui in altis habitat; et humilia respicit in caelo et in terra? Suscitans a terra inopem; et de stercore erigens pauperem. Ut collocet eum cum principibus; cum principibus populi sui. Qui habitare facit sterilem in domo; matrem filiorum laetantem.

In exitu Israel de Aegypto; domus Iacob de populo barbaro. Facta est Iudaea sanctificatio eius; Israel potestas eius. Mare vidit et fugit; Iordanis conversus est retrorsum. Montes exultaverunt ut arietes; et colles sicut agni ovium. Quid est tibi mare quod fugisti; et tu Iordanis quia conversus es retrorsum? Montes exultastis sicut arietes; et colles sicut agni ovium? A facie Domini mota est terra; a facie Dei Iacob. Qui convertit petram in stagna aquarum; et rupem in fontes aquarum. Non nobis Domine non nobis; sed nomini tuo da gloriam. Super misericordia tua et veritate tua; nequando dicant gentes ubi est Deus eorum? Deus autem noster in caelo; omnia quaecumque voluit fecit. Simulacra gentium argentum et aurum; opera manuum hominum. Os habent et non lo-

XVI

APULEJUS

AMOR UND PSYCHE

MIT SECHS RADIERUNGEN

VON FELIX HOFFMANN

ERSCHIENEN

IM VERLAG ARS LIBRORUM

GOTTHARD DE BEAUCLAIR

FRANKFURT AM MAIN

MCMLXIII

no. 49

no. 61

no. 55

Set in Aldus, a typeface designed by Hermann Zapf (Gotthard de Beauclair was instrumental in the conception of this font). Offset lithography on Mohawk Superfine paper by Capital Offset, Concord, NH. Binding by Acme Bookbinding, Charlestown, MA. Hahnemühle cover paper supplied by Atlantic Papers, Ivyland, PA. Designed by Jerry Kelly, New York City.